Safari Punctuation

a pleasant and educational trip through Punctuation Country

Written and illustrated by Mario Risso
with a great deal of writing from Marge Truzz
and writing assistance from Nancy Risso.

PASSPORT BOOKS
a division of *NTC Publishing Group*
Lincolnwood, Illinois USA

Also available: Safari Grammar

1991 Printing

Published by Passport Books, a division of NTC Publishing Group.
© 1990 by NTC Publishing Group, 4255 West Touhy Avenue,
Lincolnwood (Chicago), Illinois 60646-1975 U.S.A.
Manufactured in the United States of America.

1 2 3 4 5 6 7 8 9 TS 9 8 7 6 5 4 3 2

To the student

Have you ever been on a safari? A safari is a hunting expedition, usually in Africa. If you are on a safari, you would like to discover something. People on a traditional safari would like to discover where a wild animal—maybe a lion—is.

Discovery is what *Safari Punctuation* is all about, but you will discover something much different than African animals. *Safari Punctuation* will lead you on a journey through the rules of punctuation. (Certainly less dangerous than lions, and tigers, and bears, but just as exciting!)

Punctuation marks and capital letters are the tools you use in writing clear sentences. When you speak, the tone of your voice helps the listener understand your thoughts. *Safari Punctuation* shows you how punctuation marks and capital letters do in writing what the voice does in speaking. You will discover all the important punctuation marks and learn when, how, and why to use each mark through clearly illustrated rules and examples.

By the way, safaris usually have guides—experts who "know the way" and can instruct and advise. *Safari Punctuation* has guides, such as Jungle Jack, who are guaranteed to make your journey pleasant and rewarding. These guides will help you understand the basic rules of punctuation, and these rules will help you write clearly. So relax, meet your guides, and enjoy the journey.

Foreword

Jungle Jack and his entourage of
creatures—alligators, frogs, storks, snakes,
rabbits—may not be typical guides through
the rules of punctuation, but in this
original book they prove themselves to be
informative, entertaining companions as
they explain the characteristics of commas,
periods, question marks, exclamation
points, colons, semicolons, hyphens,
dashes, apostrophes, quotation marks,
parentheses, and capital letters.

Safari Punctuation leads students
cheerfully through the uses of all these
marks of punctuation. Its delightful
illustrations serve as functional teaching
aids that reinforce punctuation rules. These
stimulating cartoons will engage students'
interest and help them understand the
importance of using correct punctuation to
write clearly.

Students of English will enjoy this refreshing introduction to the rules of punctuation. Native speakers will find this book an entertaining way to reacquaint themselves with the basic rules of punctuation and to review the various uses of punctuation marks and capital letters.

Rules for when, how, and why to use each mark of punctuation are clearly explained and reinforced through lively examples. Entertaining dialogues between the creatures provide further clarification. A wealth of exercises enable students to practice using punctuation rules and capital letters to express themselves clearly in written English. In addition, an index is included for easy reference.

For beginners, *Safari Punctuation* provides the ideal way to stimulate students' interest while introducing them to punctuation basics. For other learners, both in and out of the classroom, *Safari Punctuation* can be used as an eye-opener—a book with real personality that will reacquaint students with the uses of punctuation through vividly illustrated rules.

Contents

Commas....................................6
   In lists...............................12
   In compound sentences/between verbs..14
   In quotations/to set off words.........20
   In dates/numbers/letters.............27
Periods..................................34
Question Marks...........................40
Exclamation Points.......................46
Colons...................................51
Semicolons...............................58
Hyphens..................................62
   To connect words....................66
   In dividing syllables...............72

Dashes................... 74
Apostrophes............. 78
   To show possession..... 80
   In contractions........ 84
Quotation Marks........ 88
   In dialogue........... 90
   In titles.............. 98
Parentheses........... 101
Capital Letters......... 106
Index................. 120

2

3

4

5

6

7

8

9

2. I saw a dinosaur, water, tall flowers, and tiny trees.

11

Use **commas** to separate three or more items in a list.

Example: Jungle Jack, Gator, Frog, and Snake arrived in the Valley of the Commas.

Note: When only two items are joined by a conjunction (**and, or, but**), no comma is needed.

Example: **Frog** and **Gator** rested on the hill.

EXERCISE 1

Write the following sentences on a separate piece of paper. Add commas where necessary.

1. The frog ate flies grasshoppers and a Big Mac.
2. We have traveled to Spain France Canada and Peru.
3. Chuck Mary and Tex are my favorite friends.
4. Tell Jack to bring string tape paper and scissors.
5. Sticks stones and branches blocked our way.

in the Valley of the Commas.

Use commas to separate two complete sentences joined by conjunctions (**and, or, but, yet**).

Example: Gator swam two laps of the pool, and Frog kept track of his time.

Example: Gator was about to dive, but then he decided against it.

Use commas to separate a list of three or more verbs*

Example: Frog marched, played the tuba, and waved.

Note: The name of the person doing the action, Frog, appears only once. It is not repeated before each verb.

*Verbs are action words. In the example, the verbs are **marched, played,** and **waved.**

16

A comma is not needed when
- there are only two verbs
  and
- the name of the doer is not repeated.*

Frog **marched** and
played the tuba.

*Frog marched, and she played the tuba. (The doer **is** repeated here.)

Study these examples. They summarize what we have just learned about commas.

Compound sentences

On vacation Snake took a balloon ride, and he played his guitar.

List of three verbs

On vacation Snake took a balloon ride, played his guitar, and watched the bird.

Two verbs only, with doer not repeated (no comma)

On vacation Snake took a balloon ride and played his guitar.

Read what's on my balloon.

It's exercise time.

EXERCISE 2

Write the following sentences on a separate piece of paper. Add commas where needed.

1. We found the road but we lost the map.
2. I went to the store came home and then returned to the store.
3. Jack ate sandwiches and drank from his canteen.
4. Sue started the campfire and Sal put up the tent.
5. We found a treasure map but none of us could understand it.
6. Tom likes checkers Dick likes puzzles and Harry likes chess.
7. We watched waited and held our breath.
8. Monkeys have an abundance of energy but sloths are usually tired.
9. The musician pounded a drum and blew on a flute.
10. Jungles are wet but deserts are dry.

19

Use commas to set off words in quotation marks.

"I don't think Frog'll jump through the flaming hoop," said Jungle Jack.

Jungle Jack repeated, "I don't think Frog'll jump through the hoop."

"I really don't think," insisted Jungle Jack, "that Frog'll jump."

Use commas to set off the name of a person spoken to.

21

Use commas to set off the words **well, no, yes,** and **oh** when these words begin a sentence.

Exercise time for everyone—even the **famous.**

EXERCISE 3

Write the following sentences on a separate piece of paper. Add the missing commas.

1. Gator said ''My best friends are crocodiles.''
2. Oh I forgot my mosquito net!
3. ''We'll be there'' said Tessa.
4. Close the tent flap Harry!
5. ''I'll buy everything'' said Jack ''that you have.''
6. No Frog isn't here.
7. ''Life in the jungle can be difficult'' said Stanley.
8. Be careful with those glass slippers Cinderella.
9. Please Wilson show me the way.
10. Well I'm ready if you are Edna.

23

Use commas to set off words that give additional information about a person, place, or thing.

Gator, the famous magician, did amazing tricks.

24

Use commas whenever the reader might be confused about the meaning of a sentence.

When Gator called, Snake was eating.

Better than: When Gator called Snake was eating.

Use commas to separate the name of a city from the name of a state or a country.

Note: If the name is in the middle of a sentence, put a comma after the last part.

San Francisco, California

Frog went to San Francisco, California, on a field trip.

Use commas to separate parts of dates.

Note: If the date is in the middle of a sentence, put a comma after the last part.

On Thursday, December 25, 1999, Gator will wear a red outfit.

27

Use commas to separate numbers: thousands, millions, billions, and so on.

Examples: 1,000   2,070,341   57,634,821,392*

*There is a comma every three numbers if you start counting from the right.

Use a comma after the opening of a friendly letter.

Note: This is the "Dear" part.

Use a comma after the closing part of any letter.

Note: This is often "Sincerely" or "Very truly yours."

Dear Snake,
I'm still learning about commas. I guess you are too. Jungle Jack said we'll soon be leaving the Valley of the Commas. I hope so!
Sincerely,
Frog

Oh, goodie! Another comma exercise.

EXERCISE 4

Write the following sentences on a separate piece of paper. Add the missing commas.

1. Fred the famous Finnish chef cooked a great meal.
2. Columbus discovered America on Friday October 12 1492.
3. There are 1000000 birds on that island.
4. Jungle Jack arrived in Cairo Egypt on August 8 1990.
5. In the picture books were stacked to the ceiling.
6. July 4 1776 is an important date in American history.
7. On Monday May 1 we will leave for New York New York.
8. Saint Augustine the oldest city in the United States is in Florida.
9. When feeding my cat likes to be left alone.
10. Dear Jack
      We'll meet you at the oasis.
        Very truly yours
        Frog and Snake

*Another way of saying "Let's do it!"

33

The **period** marks the end of a sentence.

Example: We stopped at the edge of the cliff.

35

Use periods after abbreviations.

Mr. Gator works for
Crocodile Toothbrush Co.
and lives on Everglade
Ave. in Orlando.

Common Abbreviations

With names: Mr. Mrs. Ms.

With addresses: St. (Street) Ave. (Avenue) Blvd. (Boulevard)

With organizations: Co. (Company) Inc. (Incorporated)

With days of the week:
Sun. Mon. Tues. Wed. Thurs. Fri. Sat.

With months:
Jan. Feb. Mar. Apr.
Aug. Sept. Oct. Nov. Dec.

With time expressions: A.M. P.M. A.D. B.C.

Use periods after initials in a name.

Use periods with decimals.

B.B.B. Gator (Big, Bad, and
Beautiful Gator)

Snake Sale
$8.75

Decimals:
6.2   7.25

It's time for your study **period.**

Oh, brother!*

EXERCISE 5

Write the following sentences on a separate piece of paper. Add periods where needed.

1. The period marks the end of a sentence
2. Mrs Ellison has worked for Worldwide Co two years
3. Eight dollars and eighty-eight cents equals $888
4. Mark Twain's real name was Samuel L Clemens
5. My solution was 25 and Jack's was 14 Ms Jonas, our teacher, said both solutions were correct
6. At the top of the crumpled letter was written Sept 25
7. Do Mr Laurel and Mr Hardy have their footprints in cement on Hollywood Blvd in Los Angeles, California?
8. Is 12 AM noon or midnight?
9. History says that Rome was founded in 509 BC
10. This marks the end of our study of the period

*Frog is expressing disgust at Jungle Jack's corny pun—associating "study period" and a "period."

Our safari continues...
past the Valley of the Commas...
beyond the Period Rock...

40

41

The **question mark** is used after a
direct question.

The **exclamation point** is used at the end of a sentence that expresses surprise, a strong feeling, or a command.

command   surprise   strong feeling

But first, do this!

EXERCISE 7

Write the following kinds of sentences on a separate piece of paper.

- three sentences expressing surprise
- three sentences expressing a strong feeling
- three commands

Be sure to use exclamation points.

49

50

The **colon** introduces a list.

Example:

The safari was made up of the following individuals:

Jungle Jack   Gator   Frog   Snake

The **colon** is also used before a long list of statements.

A successful safari must contain the following conditions: You must choose your companions wisely; you must take only necessary provisions; planning a route is very important; poor plans could result in possible disaster, blah-blah-blah-blah-blah.

Colons are also used . . .

between numbers telling hours and minutes

Ladies and Gentlemen:

Let this letter serve as an introduction of that esteemed explorer, Mr. Snake.

Sincerely,

Snake

in the opening of a business letter

Sir:

Dear Mr. President:

EXERCISE 8

Write the following sentences on a separate piece of paper. Add the missing colons. Also add the missing periods and commas.

1. We need the following for the party paper plates cups plastic forks and funny paper hats
2. We searched from morning to 200 PM for a four-leaf clover and we've only found these items two old shoes a key and three pennies
3. Dear Sir or Madam
   The annual stockholders' meeting for Explorers Unlimited will be held at 1030 in the morning on Dec 3 Please be present

   Very truly yours
   The Director

Anyone for exercise?

57

Use a **semicolon** between two sentences in place of the following conjunctions: **and, or, but.**

Example (with a conjunction):

Snake blocked the kick, **and** Frog blocked Gator.

Example (with a semicolon):

Snake blocked the kick; Frog blocked Gator.

59

Use a **semicolon** when items in a list contain commas.

Example:

The shops on Main Street belong to Frog, a chef; Gator, a carpenter; and Snake, a plumber.

EXERCISE 9

On a separate piece of paper, write the following:

- two sentences that are separated by a semicolon
- a sentence like the one on page 60 (Note: I said ''like,'' not the same as.)

62

The **hyphen** connects words that go together.
The hyphen is used . . .

great-granddaughter

son-in-law

to connect two or more words that represent a single idea

The hyphen is used. . . .

an up-to-date
fashion

between two or more words that go
together and come before a noun*
Examples:
a fast-growing plant
a slow-paced game
a hard-hitting policy

*Name of a person, place, or thing

The hyphen is used...

a two-foot-tall
snake

when combining numbers with other
words before nouns
Examples:
a forty-foot ladder
a four-o'clock swim
a 100-yard dash

68

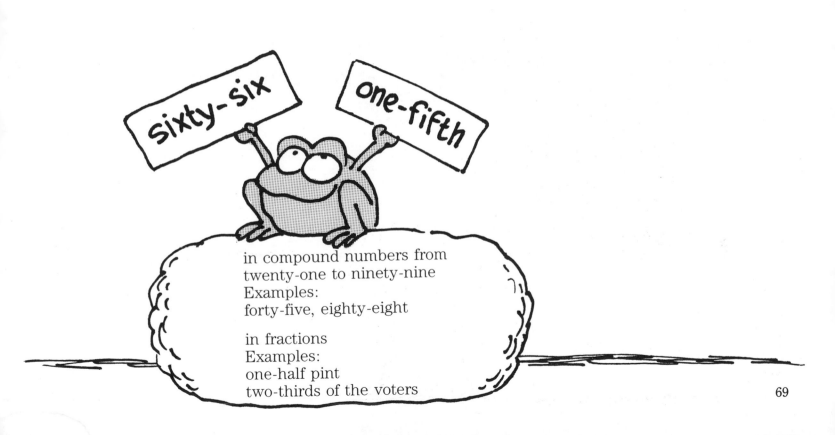

in compound numbers from
twenty-one to ninety-nine
Examples:
forty-five, eighty-eight

in fractions
Examples:
one-half pint
two-thirds of the voters

69

The hyphen is also used...

It's Snake!

Hooray for Snake!

well-known snake

in words containing **well**
Examples:
a well-built house
a well-to-do person
a well-informed leader

self-confident person

in words containing **self**
Examples:
self-respect
self-made
self-reliant

EXERCISE 10

Write the following sentences on a separate piece of paper. Add the missing hyphens.

1. Her great grandson is my brother in law.
2. Twenty foot tall waves splashed against the shore.
3. Only two fifths of the freshman class registered for the orientation lectures.
4. About one tenth of the workers in our town are self employed.
5. Forty five people began the safari.
6. The well liked student was elected class vice president.
7. A double spaced paper is easier to read than a single spaced paper.
8. My sister and brother in law live in Fairbanks.
9. The philosopher said, ''Seek advice on hard to do problems; it's not necessary to be self reliant.''
10. Who ran the first four minute mile?

The hyphen is also used...

con-tem-pla-tive

to show where to divide words
into syllables
Examples:
in-tel-li-gence
re-flec-tive
de-lib-er-a-tive

between letters when spelling
words
Examples:
s-a-f-a-r-i
p-u-n-c-t-u-a-t-i-o-n

EXERCISE 11

On a separate piece of paper, write the following words, dividing them into syllables. Use the dictionary to help you.
Example:
computer   com-pu-ter

1. location
2. inhabit
3. absence
4. Mississippi
5. composition
6. complete
7. economy
8. discount
9. expression
10. extravagant

73

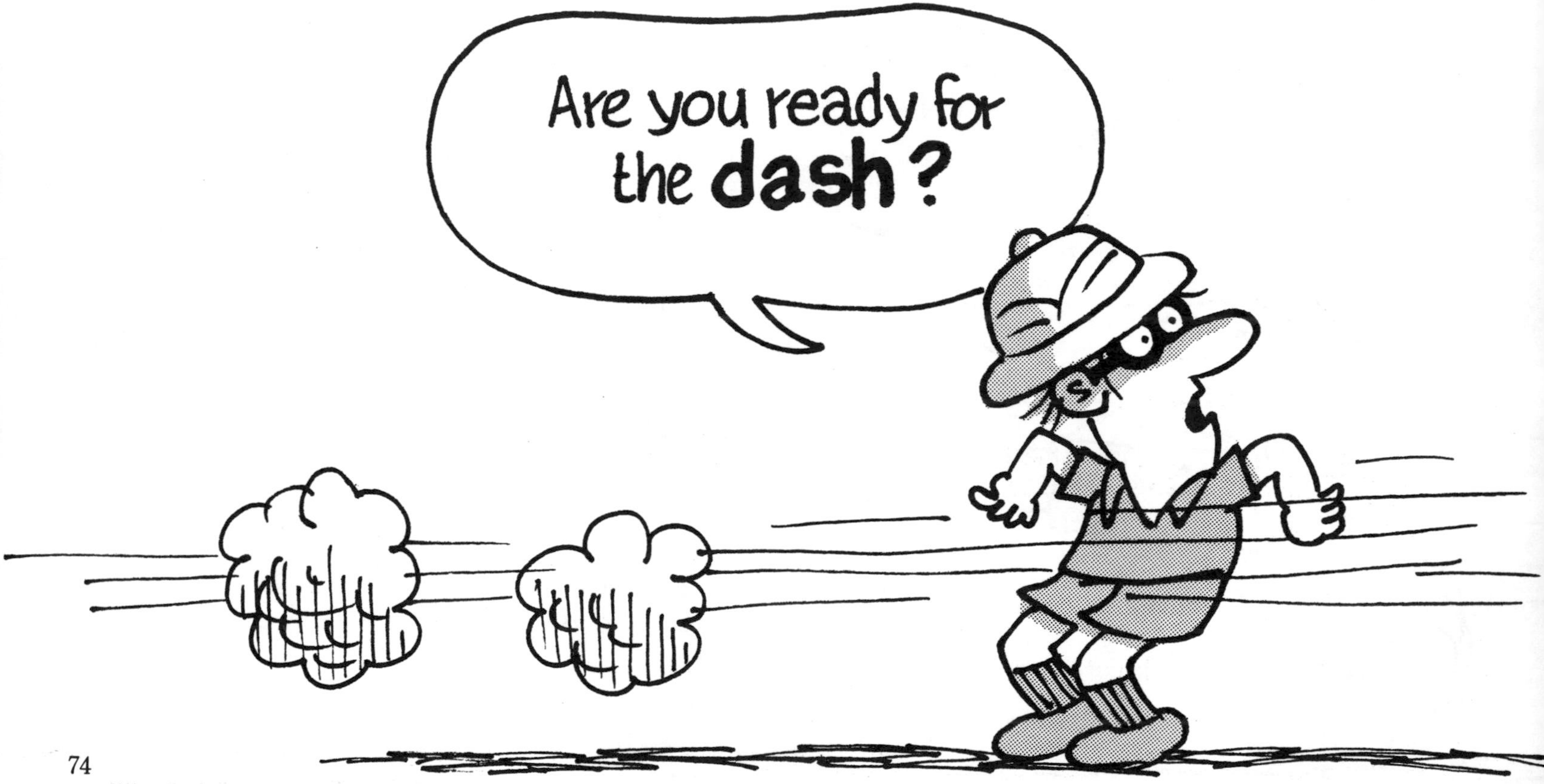
Are you ready for the **dash**?

75

The **dash** shows an abrupt change in thought.

Example:
Gator ate all the cheese at supper—or was it butter?

The dash is about three times as long as a hyphen.

EXERCISE 12

On a separate piece of paper, write two examples of sentences with abrupt changes in thought (like the one on page 76). Use dashes in the sentences.

Dash over here and do this exercise!

*The apostrophe is the mark (') between the **t** and **s** of **what's.**

Apostrophes indicate possession. Possession means ''belonging to.''

Add **'s** to a singular* noun to make it possessive.

the snake**'s** hat

Note: With compound nouns (more than one noun), add **'s** after only the last word of the name. Example: the Queen of England's crown

*Singular means telling about **one**.

For a plural* noun, add an apostrophe after the **s** to make the noun possessive.

the snake**s'** hats

*Plural means more than one. Plural nouns usually end in **s**.

When two names are connected by **and** or **or**, add **'s** only after the second name to show both own the object together.

Gator and Jungle Jack**'s** skis

82

However, if they each own an object separately, add **'s** after each name.

Gator**'s** and Jungle Jack**'s** skis

EXERCISE 13

Write the following sentences on a separate piece of paper. Add apostrophes where needed.

1. Jungle Jacks skis were on backwards.
2. The explorers task was to find where the river began. (more than one explorer)
3. The explorers meal was a can of beans. (one explorer only)
4. A players turn ends when he or she can't spell a word.
5. Gators and Jungle Jacks tents were pitched on the very top of the hill.
6. Barry and Harrys sports shop is on Fast Track Lane.
7. The six cats meows all sound alike to me.
8. Juan and Marias house is empty this week.
9. Only one students paper had no mistakes in punctuation.
10. Janets, Janes, and Jannas cars are fast.

83

Apostrophes are used with contractions.

A contraction is a shortened form of a word or word group. The apostrophe is used in place of the omitted letter(s).

Examples of contractions with the word **not**:
(Notice the letter **o** is omitted.)

cannot = can't
could not = couldn't
will not = won't
would not = wouldn't
do not = don't
does not = doesn't

*He did it because **can't** is a contraction.

Study these contractions.

Here are more contractions to study.

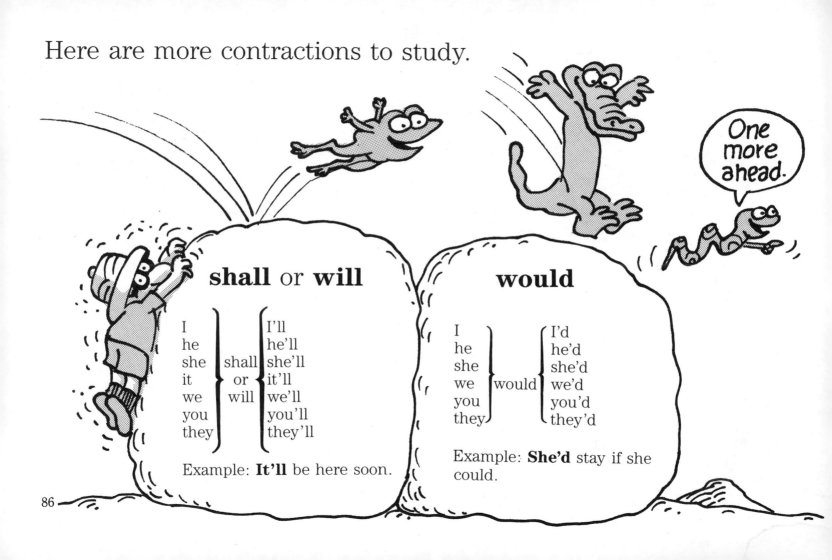

One more ahead.

shall or **will**

I		I'll
he		he'll
she	shall	she'll
it	or	it'll
we	will	we'll
you		you'll
they		they'll

Example: **It'll** be here soon.

would

I		I'd
he		he'd
she		she'd
we	would	we'd
you		you'd
they		they'd

Example: **She'd** stay if she could.

EXERCISE 14

Write the following sentences on a separate piece of paper, changing the underlined words to contractions.

Example:
I am going to Denver.
I'm going to Denver.

1. They would like to join our safari.
2. I will do this.
3. I will not do that.
4. He cannot find his new colored shoelaces.
5. They have found his shoelaces under the bed.
6. He is happy that he has found his shoelaces.
7. We are going to have a picnic.
8. They will be late if they do not hurry.
9. What is the shortest way to the lake?
10. Let us be friends.

"I can't take it anymore."

"I'm tired, do you hear, tired!"

89

''Hold on, everyone. I was just giving a dramatization of how we use **quotation marks.** They're used to enclose dialogue and conversation.''

"Is that a fact?"
said Gator.

"Do tell,"
said Frog.

"Big wow!"
exclaimed Snake.

91

Quotation marks enclose dialogue or direct conversation.

Note that only the words that are actually said are enclosed in quotation marks.

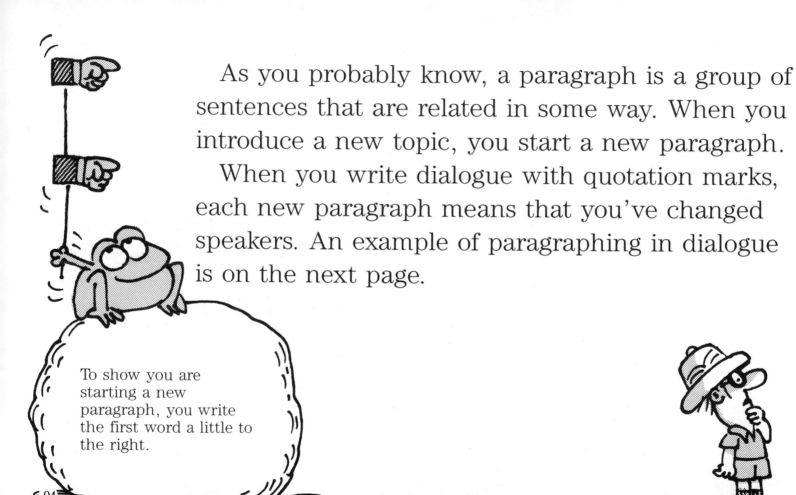

As you probably know, a paragraph is a group of sentences that are related in some way. When you introduce a new topic, you start a new paragraph.

When you write dialogue with quotation marks, each new paragraph means that you've changed speakers. An example of paragraphing in dialogue is on the next page.

To show you are starting a new paragraph, you write the first word a little to the right.

"What happened to you, Gator? Where did you get that bump?" asked Jungle Jack.

"Someone threw that ball at me. I'll bet it was Frog."

"Me! Don't be silly, Gator," said Frog. "Any fool can see Snake is the guilty party."

"Did someone call me? By the way, has anyone seen my ball?"

(Be a detective. Identify the speaker of each paragraph in the dialogue.)

Remember a comma is used to separate what is said from the phrase that identifies the speaker. When there is a question mark at the end of the quotation, no comma is needed (as in the first paragraph on this page).

"What are you thinking about?"*
asked Gator.

"A big slice of chocolate cake,"
replied Frog.

"He could at least offer us a piece,"
suggested Snake.

*When a question is asked, the comma is replaced by a question mark.

This is a quote: "It's exercise time."

EXERCISE 15

Write a story using the *Safari Punctuation* characters: Jungle Jack, Frog, Gator, and Snake. Make up a dialogue for them. Use the dialogue on page 95 as a model.

Remember to use a new paragraph when a different person speaks.

Titles of stories, songs, poems, and articles are enclosed by quotation marks. Note, however, that titles of books, movies, and magazines are underlined or italicized.*

Example:

''Blowin' in the Wind'' is a well-known song.
<u>Gone with the Wind</u> is a well-known movie.

Italics are letters that slant to the right like these. They are found in printed books. In writing or typing, underlining is used in place of italics.

''quotation marks''	<u>underlined</u> or *italicized*
songs	books
poems	movies
articles	magazines

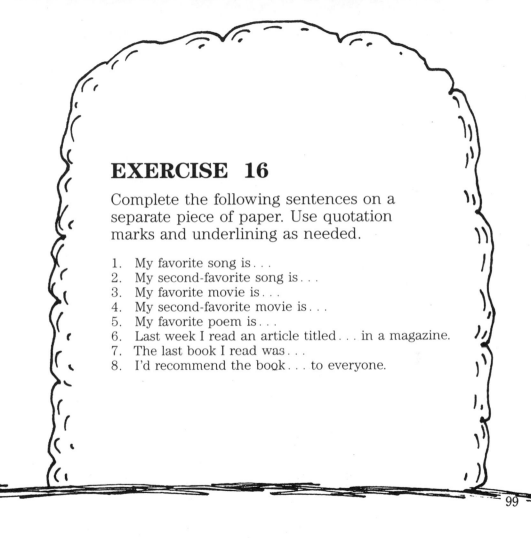

EXERCISE 16

Complete the following sentences on a separate piece of paper. Use quotation marks and underlining as needed.

1. My favorite song is...
2. My second-favorite song is...
3. My favorite movie is...
4. My second-favorite movie is...
5. My favorite poem is...
6. Last week I read an article titled... in a magazine.
7. The last book I read was...
8. I'd recommend the book... to everyone.

103

Parentheses are used to enclose related thoughts, additions, and explanations.

Jungle Jack (an amazingly fearless leader) has shown us a painless way to learn punctuation. (See all the pages in this book.)

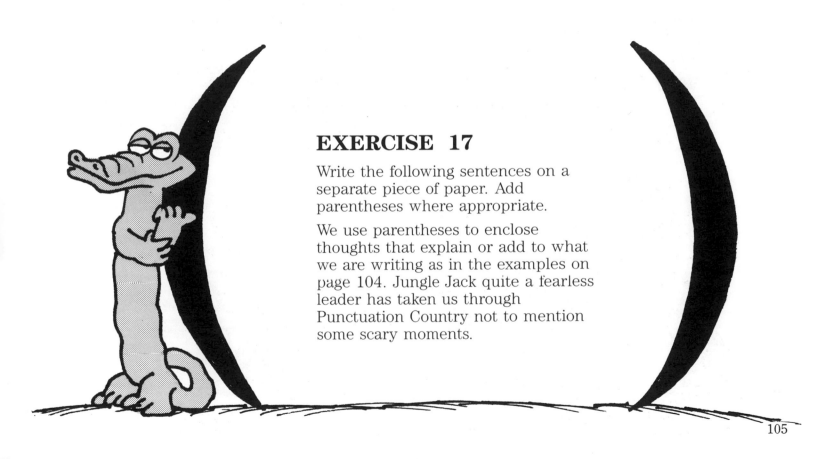

EXERCISE 17

Write the following sentences on a separate piece of paper. Add parentheses where appropriate.

We use parentheses to enclose thoughts that explain or add to what we are writing as in the examples on page 104. Jungle Jack quite a fearless leader has taken us through Punctuation Country not to mention some scary moments.

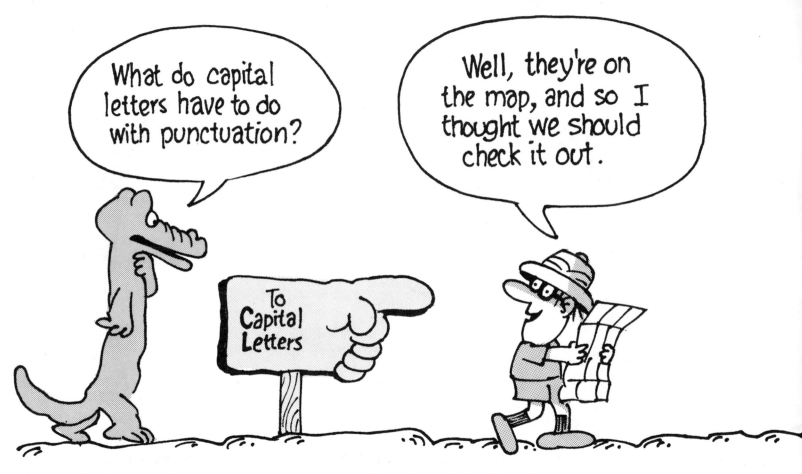

Capital and lowercase letters: A a B b C c D d E e F f G g H h I i J j K k

Capitalize the first letter of the following:

1. Proper nouns
   Examples:
   Mary, **T**ed, **S**tatue of **L**iberty

2. Personal titles used before proper nouns
   Examples:
   Doctor Jekyll, **C**aptain Kangaroo, **S**enator Smarts

3. The first word of a sentence
(**T**here is a period at the end of
this sentence.)

4. The important words in the title
of a book, movie, song, and so
on

Alice in Wonderland

Here are more capitalization rules. Capitalize . . .

5. The names of days and months
   (but **not** of seasons)

It was **M**onday, **J**anuary 23,
smack in the middle of winter.

6. The names of places

Here are more capitalization rules. Capitalize...

7. The names of languages and words relating to nationalities

8. The names of organizations, universities, clubs, companies, and so on

Here are more capitalization rules. Capitalize...

9. The first word in a direct quotation
   Example:
   The baby kangaroo said, "**I**t's time to leave home."

10. Here is a general rule. Capitalize the names of particular things.
    Example:
    Mr. **G**ator was trendy.

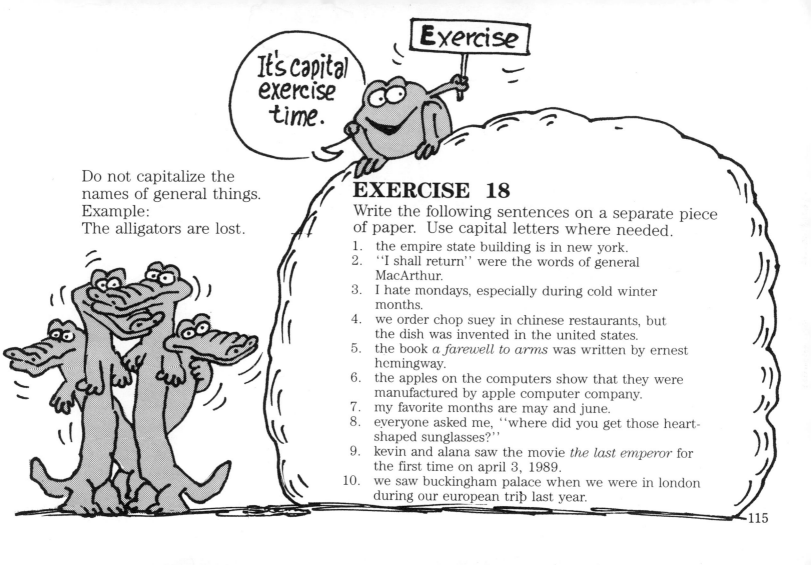

It's capital exercise time.

Exercise

Do not capitalize the names of general things.
Example:
The alligators are lost.

EXERCISE 18

Write the following sentences on a separate piece of paper. Use capital letters where needed.

1. the empire state building is in new york.
2. "I shall return" were the words of general MacArthur.
3. I hate mondays, especially during cold winter months.
4. we order chop suey in chinese restaurants, but the dish was invented in the united states.
5. the book *a farewell to arms* was written by ernest hemingway.
6. the apples on the computers show that they were manufactured by apple computer company.
7. my favorite months are may and june.
8. everyone asked me, "where did you get those heart-shaped sunglasses?"
9. kevin and alana saw the movie *the last emperor* for the first time on april 3, 1989.
10. we saw buckingham palace when we were in london during our european trip last year.

116

118

Index

abbreviations, 36–37
apostrophes, 78–87
  in contractions, 84–87
  to indicate possession,·80–83
capitalization, 106–115
  of days, 110
  of months, 110
  of languages and nationalities, 112
  of organizations, 113
  of personal titles, 108
  of place names, 111
  of proper names, 108
  of titles of works, 109
colons, 51–57
  after the opening of letters, 56
  introducing lists, 52–55
  separating time numbers, 56
commas, 6–31
  after opening of letters, 29
  after closing of letters, 29
  after introductory words, 22
  in direct address, 21
  in dates, 27
  in numbers, 28
  in compound sentences, 14–15
  in lists, 12–13, 16
  separating verbs, 16–18
  setting off person spoken to, 21
  setting off explanations of nouns, 24
  use of, to avoid confusion, 25
  with place names, 26
  with quotations, 20, 96
  with appositives, 24
compound sentences
  use of commas to connect, 14–15
  use of semicolons to connect, 58–59
contractions, use of apostrophes with, 84–87
dashes, 74–77
dates, use of commas in, 27
exclamation points, 46–49
fractions, use of hyphens in, 69
geographical names. *See* place names
hyphens, 62–73
  in compounds with **well**, 70
  in compounds with **self**, 70

in numbers, 69
in groups of words before nouns, 67–68
in compound words, 66
in fractions, 69
in spelling words, 72
separating syllables, 72
indentation, with dialogue, 94–95
initials, periods with, 38
italics, 98
in titles, 98–99
letters
use of colons in opening, 56
use of commas in closing, 29
use of commas in opening, 29
lists
commas in, 12–13, 16
semicolons in, 60
numbers
use of commas with numbers, 28
use of colons with numbers, 53
use of hyphens in spelled-out numbers, 69
parentheses, 101–105
periods, 34–39
after abbreviations, 36–37
after initials, 38

at end of sentences, 34–35
with decimals, 38
personal titles, capitalization of, 108
place names
capitalization of, 111
use of commas with, 26
proper names, capitalization of, 108
question marks, 40–43
quotation marks, 88–99
in titles, 98–99
in dialogue, 90–97
quotations
capitalization of, 114
commas in, 20, 96
semicolons, 58–61
connecting sentences, 58–59
in lists, 60
sentences, compound. *See* compound sentences
sentences, punctuation at end of,
exclamation points, 48–49
periods, 34–35
question marks, 42–43
titles of works
capitalization of, 109
italics or quotation marks with, 98